My Mini-Micro
Mindset
Manual

♥ Neeta Oza

Hashtag PRESS

Published in Great Britain by Hashtag Press 2019

A CIP catalogue for this book is available from the British
Library.

ISBN 978-1-9998053-8-8

Typeset in Garamond Classic 11.25/14 by Blaze Typesetting

Printed in Great Britain by Clays Ltd, Elcograf S.p.A.

Hashtag PRESS

HASHTAG PRESS BOOKS
Hashtag Press Ltd
Kent, England, United Kingdom
Email: info@hashtagpress.co.uk
Website: www.hashtagpress.co.uk
Twitter: @hashtag_press

To the one who has always supported me,
unconditionally, during the most important
—as well as the most absolutely ridiculous—
times of my life.
This is for you—a shining light!
I hope you enjoy it Mum.
Love you x

Hello!

I'm going to start by thanking you for reading my new book. This makes me really happy and emotional.

Yes, this is a manual, written just for you! It can also be considered a reference guide, which I'm still learning from and always will be! I hope you'll keep it close by, so you have it to hand whenever you feel you need a bit of support, guidance or reassurance.

Working on yourself is a lifelong journey and I've repeatedly felt lost and anxious. I've negatively fallen down three steps, yet I've always come back ten steps forward – somehow with laughter, determination and an inner energy, which is beyond me, yet I know is within ALL of us.

So, it's time to embrace this blessed life experience. Something I haven't always done. Something I sometimes forget about. I always presume that my next breath and heartbeat will arrive, not registering that the gift of life can end in a flash. Just like that. On a lighter note (!) I hope you enjoy this book about mindset, as much as I enjoyed creating it, and I'm truly grateful that you're even reading this introduction. I hope this manual helps you to take a breath and pause.

Lots of love, Neeta x

The Easy

A to Z

A is for Attraction

Having the kind of outlook that Attracts the best of the best. This involves as much positivity as possible, rays of sunshine and lots of laughter.

And always be Attracted to yourself.

B is for Belief

Believing in something positive—something of a higher purpose. It could be the Universe, nature, God, religion, or a person, perhaps even just a simple mantra.

But always, always Believe in yourself.

C is for Care

Taking good, proper Care of yourself is vital. Remember, there is only one of you!

A lovely doctor once told me, "Eat well, exercise well, relax well, sleep well," and I've tried to do just that ever since.

D is for Dedication

Staying Dedicated to yourself, your purpose, and your gift of life.

What are you Dedicated to achieving today?

E is for Energy

Keeping a continuous, vibrant flow of Energy in everything you do. Be conscious of making the most of every moment. It can be from simple things such as washing-up the dishes or going to the gym, to simply sitting and reading a great book (like you're doing now).

F is for Fun & Fitness

Having as much Fun in life as possible! Yes, there will be days when you just want to reflect, sit on the sofa, binge-watch Netflix and eat chocolate (which can be bloomin' good Fun in itself).

Whatever you do, just enjoy every moment.

Fitness is a dear part of my life and so I'm dedicating a mini-micro section to it, with some of my favourite forms of the F word. If you can always feel the Fun, Flexibility and Flow of Fitness, I think you're definitely on to a winner.

F is for Fun & Fitness

Cycling

Whether it's a spin class, or riding a bike outdoors, they both remind me of my Girl-Racer BMX days. Great memories.

F is for Fun & Fitness

Dancing

It doesn't really matter how or where you Dance.
Hit the club or your kitchen floor and always with
your favourite tunes on—of course!

F is for Fun & Fitness

Pilates

Keeps your core and spine divine. Also keeps them united as Best-Friends-Forever.

F is for Fun & Fitness

Walking

Ideally in nature. Walk as slowly as possible. Soothe your brain. No traffic. No weaving. No mobile phone. No rush.

F is for Fun & Fitness

Weights

Try lifting, even for a few minutes a day. It doesn't matter if you have proper Weights or bean cans. Load your bones and feel strong—inside and out.

F is for Fun & Fitness

Yoga

Syncs your mind. Syncs your body. It's an assured way to get your breathing in-check.

Ǧ is for Giving

Giving as much to yourself as possible in order to have the energy to give to others. Be conscious of Giving away your power at the same time! Focus on yourself first. You matter.

H is for Health

Putting your Health first; numero uno, head honcho. Feeling full of life and keeping on-the-go; yet taking valuable time to heal and re-energise whenever you feel it's necessary.

Health is physical, mental; and always emotional.

I is for Ideas

Keep them coming. Whatever they may be. Write them down. Action them if you can. Keep dreaming and don't limit yourself.

Ideas make the world go round.

J is for JOY

Life is going to throw some really bad stuff your way. Seriously bad. But staying Joyful throughout, as much as possible, is going to make things that tad bit easier. It's hard to remain this way when faced with the bad times, yet it's damn rewarding when you come out stronger the other side!

Don't ever let anyone steal your Joy.

K is for Kindness

Being as Kind as you can—to yourself to start with.
You are your base, your foundation. From there,
being Kind to everyone else, as much as possible,
is an easier progression.

It's one of the most rewarding feelings in the world!

L is for Love & Laughter

Love is the question, the message and the answer. Start with self-love and take it from there.

Laughter is the absolute key to life. Looking back, Laughter can heal most 'situations.' Laughing your way through life is the way forward.

M is for Mindset

Having a positive Mindset, which will keep you getting up and moving forwards, no matter how many times you fall down.

Listening to amazing speakers such as Christie Marie Sheldon, Les Brown, Marisa Peer, Earl Nightingale and Abraham Hicks helps me immensely.

N is for saying 'No!'

Remembering that it's OK to just say 'No' when you really need to put yourself first. Everything with balance!

☉ is for Ongoing

Being the best person you can be at that time.
Ongoing.

All day.

Every-Damn-Day.

P is for Power

Reclaiming your Power by releasing the past and future and focusing on the present. When was the last time you checked in to realign yourself?

You should do it. Every. Single. Day. As many times as you need to.

Q is for Q-Tip

Keeping yourself polished and ready for the Game of Life!

R

R is for Relaxation

Always listen to your body and take the time to chill and Relax. It could be a walk, a spa break, reading a book or just sitting in silence, so that you can re-energise and be the best you can be. We ultimately want to avoid burnout.

S is for Smiling

The most attractive thing about someone—and the best first impression—is a big cheesy Smile. Go on, show us your pearly whites!

T is for Time

Time is precious. Make the most of the Time that is here now. Think about how precious every breath and heartbeat is. Don't waste your Time on anything that doesn't bring you joy.

U is for Under Construction

We're always going to be a work in progress. Everyone is Under Construction. And that's fine! As long as you're trying as hard as you can, then you're doing a fantastic job.

V is for Vibrancy

Keep fresh and stay Vibrant. Raise the Vibration so that you can make space; where the air is clear, open and receptive for new, positive, exciting things.

Ẇ is for Wealth

Health is the highest Wealth. Cherish it always.
Knowing that financial Wealth is to be embraced
and is just an exchange; that is all.

X is for Ex-Power

Releasing any power that you once gave away frivolously. Giving mental love to the Exes—past partners, past jobs, past thoughts, past regrets. Moving on—amicably and with love—towards a brighter, lighter, amazing journey.

Y is for saying 'Yes!'

Shout a big, resounding 'Yes!' to as many things as possible—with balance, of course. Live your life to the absolute fullest without compromising your health.

Z

Z is for Zzzzz

Catching those Zeds, and healing, recovering and re-energising, whilst you sleep. Get your mind, body and soul in order, so that you wake-up ready to live and embrace the Gift of Life.

About the Author

Neeta wrote her first book at the age of three with coloured paper, crayons and an array of partially-life-like drawings of her family which always made her Mum laugh. Thirty-seven years later, she finally published her first (real) book with Hashtag Press.

In 2000, Neeta joined a gym and—feeling the benefits of keeping fit—qualified as a Yoga Instructor in 2011, then a Pilates Instructor in 2017. She vowed at twenty-five years old, during a Chinese meal with friends, to stay in the best physical shape once she reached forty; and ever since has been trying to stay in the best mental shape too.

A fourteen-minute Law of Attraction YouTube clip changed her life for the better in 2016. This led to her viewing multiple motivational speakers, and also prompted the creation of this book.

With an ever-expanding love for health and wellbeing, Neeta delved into the world of mindset and simple ways to alleviate stress during modern life. Through 'My Mini-Micro Mindset Manual' Neeta hopes to inspire and be inspired by anyone interested in maintaining an optimistic outlook during the rollercoaster called life!

Find out more at www.neetafitness.com
Follow on Twitter, Instagram & Facebook @neetafitness